DK Kids' First
COOK
book

ANGELA WILKES
HELEN DREW

DK

LONDON, NEW YORK, MUNICH,
MELBOURNE and DELHI

Editor Jane Elliot
Series Editor Helen Drew and Angela Wilkes
Design Mathewson Bull
Art Director Roger Piddy
Photography Dave King and David Johnson
Illustration Brian Delf
Managing Editor Jane Yorke
Managing Art Editor Chris Scollen
Home Economists Dolly Meers and Jane Suthering

For 2012 edition
Senior Editor Ros Walford
Production Editor Kavita Varma
Senior Production Controller Claire Pearson

DK Delhi
Editorial Manager Glenda Fernandes
Editor Pankhoori Sinha
Art Director Shefali Upadhyay
Designers Neerja Rawat,
Mitun Banerjee
DTP Designer Harish Aggarwal

This edition published in 2012
First published in Great Britain in 1999 by
Dorling Kindersley Limited, 80 Strand,
London WC2R ORL

This edition published for The Book People Ltd,
Hall Wood Avenue, Haydock, St. Helens WA11 9UL

© 1999, 2012 Dorling Kindersley Limited, London
Penguin Group (UK)

10 9 8 7 6 5 4 3 2 1
001-186083-Feb/12

Projects originally published in
My First Cook Book (1989, 2007)
My First Baking Book (1992, 2008)

A CIP catalogue record for this book is available
from the British Library.

ISBN 978-1-4093-8431-1

Colour reproduction by Colourscan, Singapore
Printed and bound by Leo Paper Products Ltd, China

**Discover more at
www.dk.com**

CONTENTS

cooking by pictures

DK Kids' First Cook Book shows you step-by-step how to make and bake all sorts of delicious things to eat. The easy-to-follow recipes show you which ingredients you need, what to do with them, and what the finished food should look like – life size! There are lots of great ideas too for creating fun and colourful decorations. Below are the points to look for in each recipe and opposite is an important list of cook's rules to read before you start.

How to use this book

The ingredients
The ingredients you need for each recipe are shown clearly so you can see if you have the right amounts.

Increasing the quantity
Each recipe tells you how many treats the ingredients make. To make more, double or treble the quantities.

Cook's tools
These illustrated checklists show you which utensils you need to have ready before you start cooking.

sweet and savoury scones

Here you can find out how to make sweet scones, fruit scones, and cheese scones. The ingredients shown will make about ten scones. Below you can see how to make sweet, fruit, and cheese scone doughs. Turn the page to find out how to cut out and fill your scones.

You will need

120 ml (4 fl oz) milk

225 g (8 oz) self raising flour

25 g (1 oz) caster sugar

50 g (2 oz) sultanas

50 g (2 oz) grated cheddar cheese

50 g (2 oz) softened butter

A pinch of salt

COOK'S TOOLS
Baking tray, Wire rack, Mixing bowl, Whisk, 6 circular cutters, Measuring jug, Rolling pin, Sharp knife, Cheese grater, Pastry brush, Wooden spoon

making scone dough

1. Set the oven to 425°F/220°C/ Gas Mark 7. Put the flour and salt in the mixing bowl. Add the butter and cut it into pieces.

2. Rub the butter and flour together with your fingertips until the mixture looks like breadcrumbs. Stir in the sugar.

3. Add the milk to the mixture and stir everything together with the wooden spoon to make a smooth mixture.

fruit scones

4. Knead the mixture by pressing and squeezing it together with your hands until you have formed a stiff dough.

5. Follow the recipe for sweet scones but add the sultanas to the mixture after you have stirred in the sugar.

cheese scones

6. Follow the same recipe for sweet scones, but add the grated cheese instead of the caster sugar before you add the milk.

42

43

cook's rules

1. Remember you must always have an adult with you before you cook or bake anything.
2. Read each recipe before you start, to make sure you have everything you need.
3. Wash your hands and put on an apron before you start.
4. Carefully weigh or measure all the ingredients you use.
5. Always wear oven gloves when touching anything hot, or when using the oven.
6. Be careful with sharp knives. and check that saucepan handles are turned away from you so that you do not knock them.
7. If you get burnt, hold the burn under cold running water immediately and call for help.
8. Never leave the kitchen when gas or electric rings are turned on.
9. Always turn the oven off when you have finished with it.

Step-by-step
Step-by-step photographs and easy instructions to follow show you what to do at each stage of the recipe.

The oven glove symbol
Whenever you see this symbol in a recipe, always put on oven gloves and ask an adult to help you.

The finished result
The picture at the end of each recipe shows the finished food life-size, and ideas for decoration.

Teatime treats

You can use different shaped biscuit cutters to make small scones, or make a big scone round with your hands. Scones taste best when warm, with or without butter. Try filling sweet or fruit scones with jam and whipped cream.

COOK'S TOOLS

Small bowl   Whisk
Sharp knife
Knife

cutting out the scones

1. Grease a baking tray. Gently roll out the dough until it is 2 cm thick. Cut out shapes with biscuit cutters dipped in flour.

2. Put the scones on a baking tray*, brush them with milk and bake for 12 to 15 minutes, until firm and risen. Cool them on a wire rack.

A scone round

3. Roll the dough into a circle 2.5 cm thick. Divide the top into eight, then brush it with milk. Bake for about 25 minutes.

Whipping the cream

4. Whisk the cream in the small bowl until it is thick. Cut the sweet or fruit scones in half and fill them with jam and cream.

*Sprinkle some extra grated cheese on top of the cheese scones.

You will need

150 ml (¼ pint) double cream

SWEET SCONES

Strawberry jam

Whipped cream

CHEESE SCONES

Jam

A FRUIT SCONE ROUND

Grated cheddar cheese sprinkled on before baking

44

45

Little cakes

Little sponge cakes are simple and quick to make. Here you can see everything you will need to make about ten small and ten tiny plain or cherry cakes. If you wish to make more, you will have to double or treble the amounts of ingredients shown. Don't forget that you will need more icing too! On the next four pages there are lots of exciting ideas for icing and decorating all your little cakes.

You will need

2 eggs

6 glacé cherries

100 g (4 oz)
soft
margarine

COOK'S TOOLS

Baking tray

Small bowl

Mixing bowl

Sieve

Bun tin

Wire rack

Paper sweet cases

2 teaspoons

Wooden spoon

Knife

Paper cases

100 g
(4 oz)
caster sugar

What to do

1. Set the oven to 180°C/ 350°F/Gas Mark 4. Put the larger paper cases in the bun tin and the sweet cases on the baking tray.

2. Sieve the self-raising flour into the mixing bowl. Add the soft margarine and the caster sugar to the flour.

100 g (4 oz) self-raising flour

3. Break the eggs into the bowl. Beat everything together with the wooden spoon until the mixture is soft and creamy.

4. To make cherry cakes, cut the glacé cherries into small pieces with a sharp knife* and stir them into the cake mixture.

5. Put two teaspoonfuls of the mixture into each larger paper case and one teaspoonful into each sweet case.

6. Bake the tiny cakes for 10 to 15 minutes and the small ones for 20 to 25 minutes. Then put them on a wire rack to cool.

*Ask an adult to help you.

7

Icing the cakes

You can make lots of different icing for your little cakes. Here you can find out how to make chocolate, white, and pink butter icing and how to colour fondant icing and mould it into shapes. Look on the next two pages for lots of decorating ideas.

You will need

100 g (4 oz) soft butter

100 g (4 oz) ready-made fondant icing

2 tablespoons cocoa powder

3 drops red food colouring

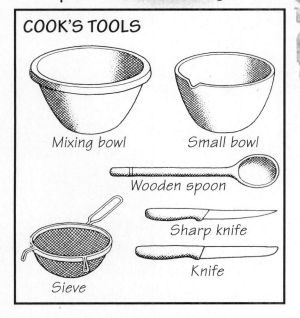

COOK'S TOOLS

Mixing bowl   Small bowl

Wooden spoon

Sharp knife

Sieve   Knife

215 g (7½ oz) icing sugar

what to do

1. Put half the butter into the mixing bowl and cut it into small pieces. Beat it with the wooden spoon until it is creamy.

2. Sift 125 g (4 oz) of icing sugar into a small bowl. Mix the sugar into the butter a little at a time until the icing is creamy.

3. Divide the icing in half. Put half of it in a small bowl. Beat the red colouring into the other half to make pink icing.

Fondant icing

4. To make chocolate icing, use 90 g (3½ oz) of icing sugar and the cocoa power and follow steps 1 and 2 above.

1. To make pink fondant icing, add 3 drops of red colouring to the fondant. Knead it until the colour is even.

2. Make a roll of fondant for the elephant's trunk and shape flat circles for its ears. Make pig's ears from flat ovals of fondant.

cakes with faces

1. Remove the cakes from their cases. Arrange the small and tiny cakes together to make faces with ears or noses or both.

2. Ice the bottom and sides of a tiny cake and stick it on top of a small cake covered with the same coloured icing.

3. When you have iced all your cakes, give them faces by decorating them with sweets and chocolates before the icing dries.

Funny faces

Little cakes are great fun to make and they look really bright and colourful as well. Look out for all sorts of different chocolates and sweets to use for decoration. Copy the butterflies, soldier, teddy bear, elephant, and other funny face cakes shown here or experiment with some ideas of your own! Why not try making funny face cakes that look like your family and pets for a special family meal or party.

You will need

Red liquorice laces

Liquorice stumps

Liquorice strips

White chocolate drops

Chocolate drops

Glacé cherries

White chocolate buttons

Chocolate buttons

Coloured chocolate sweets

Chocolate sugar strands

CHERRY CAKES

Eat your cherry cakes as they are, or iced and decorated with sweets.

Pieces of glacé cherry

BUTTERFLIES

Pink butter icing

Butter icing

Sponge wings

Cut a circle out of some small cakes and then cut the circles in half to make wings. Fill the hole in the cakes with butter or fondant icing and put a wing on either side.

PIG

Chocolate drop eyes

Pink fondant ears

Chocolate drop nostrils

Red sweet tongue

TEDDY BEAR

Tiny cake cut in half with pieces of chocolate for ears

Yellow sweet and chocolate drop eyes

Red sweet nose

Chocolate sugar strand snout

SEAL

Chocolate drop and white chocolate button eyes

RACOON

Chocolate button ears

White chocolate drop and liquorice eyes

Chocolate sugar strand fur

Liquorice on white chocolate button

Liquorice whiskers

DOG

Chocolate drop eyes

Liquorice nose

Red sweet tongue

Chocolate sugar strand whiskers

SOLDIER

Chocolate sugar strand busby

Red sweet

Red liquorice eyebrows

Chocolate drop and yellow sweet eyes

Glacé cherry nose

Red liquorice mouth

Liquorice chinstrap and moustache

ELEPHANT

Pink fondant circles on tiny cakes for ears

White chocolate drop tusks

Chocolate drop eyes

Pink fondant curled up on a tiny cake

11

Surprise cake

For birthdays, parties, and other celebrations, it is nice to make a special cake. Or you can make a cake just because you want to give someone a surprise. Here is a recipe for a delicious and light sponge cake, which you can decorate however you like. You can find out how to make the cake below, and then turn to the next two pages to see how to ice and decorate it in different ways.

You will need

150 g (6 oz)
softened butter

150 g (6 oz) plain flour

making the cake

1. Set the oven at 180°C/350°F/ Gas Mark 4. Rub some butter around the inside of the two sandwich tins thoroughly.

2. Put the softened butter and sugar in the mixing bowl. Beat them with the wooden spoon until the mixture is pale and creamy.

3. Beat the eggs in a bowl. Add them to the butter and sugar mixture a little at a time, stirring in well until it is smooth.

3 eggs

150 g (6 oz) caster sugar

1½ teaspoons baking powder

COOK'S TOOLS

Mixing bowl

Fork

Wooden spoon

2 x 20-cm (8-in) sandwich cake tins

Small bowl

Wire rack

4. Sift the flour and baking powder into the mixture and mix well. The cake mixture should be soft and light.

5. Pour half of the cake mixture into each sandwich tin and smooth it level. Place the tins in the oven for 20–25 minutes.

6. The cakes are done when well-risen and golden brown. They should be springy in the middle. Put them on a wire rack to cool.

Now turn the page.

13

Easter cake

This cake is filled and topped with chocolate butter icing and decorated. Copy the hen, or make up a new picture.

COOK'S TOOLS

Mixing bowl

Sieve

Knife

Wooden spoon

You will need

15 ml (1 tablespoon) cocoa powder

15–30 ml (1–2 tablespoons) milk

75 g (3 oz) softened butter

150 g (6 oz) icing sugar

Icing the cake

1. Put the butter in the bowl and cut it into small pieces. Beat it hard with the wooden spoon until it is soft and creamy.

2. Sift the icing sugar and cocoa powder into the bowl, a little at a time, mixing them in with the butter. Then stir in the milk.

3. When the cakes are cool, spread half the icing on one. Put the other cake on top and spread the rest of the icing over it.

Arranging the easter cake

4. Now decorate the cake. Press the sweets firmly into the icing. Start with the border, do the nest, and arrange the hen last of all.

Coloured chocolate sweets

Blanched almonds

Sugar strands

Chocolate drops

The finished cake

Almond beak

Almond tail

Chocolate drops

Brown sweet border

Coloured chocolate sweets

Sugar strands

15

A rich chocolate cake

No birthday or party is complete without a surprise cake – so here's how to make a wonderful chocolate cake that tastes delicious.

You will need

100 g (4 oz) softened butter

250 ml (8 fl oz) milk

2 large eggs

1 tablespoon lemon juice

COOK'S TOOLS

Mixing bowl

Wire rack

Greaseproof paper

Greased 22 cm deep cake tin

Pencil

Scissors

Measuring jug

Dessert spoon

Sieve

Wooden spoon

What to do

1. Set the oven to 180°C/ 350°F/Gas Mark 4. Draw round the cake tin on greaseproof paper. Cut out the circle and put it in the tin.

2. Stir the lemon juice into the milk. Put the butter and half the sugar into the mixing bowl and heat it until pale and fluffy.

250 g (9 oz)
caster sugar

1 teaspoon
bicarbonate of soda

50 g (2 oz)
cocoa powder

225 g (8 oz) plain flour

3. Beat the eggs into the mixture one at a time. Stir in the rest of the sugar. Sift the flour, soda, and cocoa powder together.

4. Beat in half the milk and fold in half the flour. Add the rest of the milk and then the rest of the flour. Mix until smooth.

5. Pour the mixture into the cake tin and bake it for one hour. Then tip the cake out of the tin and leave it on a wire rack to cool.

Healthy Muffins

Muffins are really easy and quick, and make a delicious breakfast treat. This recipe makes 12 scrumptious blueberry muffins. If you like, you can use raspberries, cherries (stoned and chopped), chopped-up apricots, or even chocolate chips instead of the blueberries. Just add them at step 3.

You will need

250 g (9 oz) self-raising flour

140 g (5 oz) golden caster sugar

150 ml (5 fl oz) milk

½ teaspoon vanilla essence

120 ml (4 fl oz) vegetable oil

1 large egg

COOK'S TOOLS

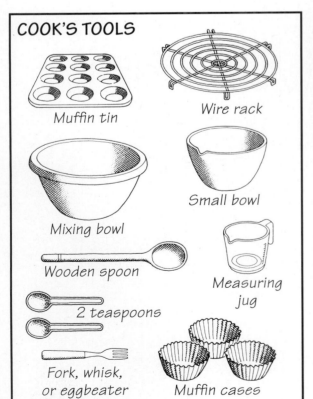

Muffin tin

Wire rack

Mixing bowl

Small bowl

Wooden spoon

Measuring jug

2 teaspoons

Fork, whisk, or eggbeater

Muffin cases

175 g (6 oz) fresh blueberries

What to do

1. Ask an adult to help you. Set the oven to 200°C/400°F/Gas Mark 6. Put the muffin cases in the muffin tin and set to one side.

2. Crack the egg in a bowl. Beat it slightly with a fork or a whisk, then mix in the milk, vanilla essence, and oil.

3. Mix the flour and sugar in another bowl. Scoop a well in the middle, then add the blueberries and pour in the wet ingredients.

4. Fold the mixture together gently in a few strokes with a wooden spoon. It does not matter if the mixture looks lumpy.

5. Spoon the mixture into the muffin cases so each case is half full, then bake for 20–25 minutes until golden brown.

Leave the muffins to cool on a wire rack

The finished muffins

Quick bread

Making bread is great fun. This recipe makes enough dough for eight rolls. Here you can see how to make the dough. The next two pages show you how to make and decorate the rolls.

You will need

1 dessertspoon
vegetable or sunflower oil

3 g (½ sachet) quick-action dried yeast

A large pinch of salt

COOK'S TOOLS

Mixing bowl

Measuring jug

Kitchen scissors

Pastry brush

Wooden spoon

Greased baking tray

Wire rack

350 g (12 oz)
strong white flour

making the dough

1. Set the oven to 230°C/ 450°F/Gas Mark 8. Put the flour, yeast, and salt in the mixing bowl. Add the vegetable oil and water.

2. Mix everything together into a firm dough. If the dough is sticky, add a little flour. Add a little water if it is too dry.

3. Put the dough on a floured table. Push your hands into it, gather it into a ball and turn it again and again for 5 minutes.

4. Shape the dough into rolls (see next page). Put them on to the greased baking tray. Then put them in a warm place*.

5. When the rolls have doubled in size, you can decorate them however you want (see the next page).

6. Bake them for 15–20 minutes. They are done if they sound hollow when tapped underneath. Put them on the wire rack to cool.

*Ask an adult for a suitable, warm place.

210 ml (³⁄₈ pint) warm water

Twist and roll

You can make bread rolls in all sorts of different shapes. You can vary them even more by using different seeds to make crunchy toppings. To make the rolls, break the bread dough into eight pieces, all about the same size, then follow the instructions on the right. Remember that the baked rolls will be twice as big as the dough, because they will grow when rising.

Tortoise roll

Stick tiny balls of dough around a roll to look like four legs, a head, and a tail. Mark the top of the roll to look like a shell.

Prickly hedgehog

Make a pointed snout shape at one end of a roll. Snip the rest of the roll, the hedgehog's body, with scissors to make prickles.

Decorating the rolls

When the rolls have risen and are ready to bake, you can decorate them with any of the ingredients shown below. To give the rolls a golden brown glaze, you will also need a beaten egg and a pastry brush.

You will need

Flower roll sprinkled with caraway seeds

Sesame seeds

Caraway seeds

Poppy seeds

Currants

1 beaten egg

Prickly hedgehog with currant eyes and nose

Brush the rolls lightly with the beaten egg. Sprinkle seeds over them and press them gently into place. The rolls are now ready to go into the oven (see the previous page).

Cottage roll sprinkled with poppy seeds

cottage roll

Make a smaller ball of dough than the others. Brush the base of it with water. Stick it to a larger roll and make a dent in the top.

Snail roll

Roll a ball of dough into a sausage shape. Brush one side of it with water and wind it into a coil, leaving one end as the head.

Flower roll

Flatten a ball of dough slightly. Snip all round the edge of the dough with kitchen scissors to make petal shapes.

The finished rolls on a cooling rack

23

Bread bears

You can make these bears using the recipe on page 20, but you need to double the ingredients given. You can also use a mixture of white and wholemeal flour. When you have made the dough, break it into three different-sized balls. Apart from the dough, you will need decorating ingredients, a large, greased baking tray, and kitchen scissors or a knife.

For decoration

1 beaten egg

Sesame seeds

Poppy seeds

Currants

Grated cheese

making the bears

1. Break a ball of dough in two. Roll half of it into a big ball for the bear's body. Put it on the baking tray and flatten it a little.

2. Break the remaining dough in two. Roll half of it into a small ball. Roll the other half into a sausage shape 15 cm (6 in) long.

3. Brush one side of the small ball with egg. Stick it to the bear's body, tucking it slightly underneath to make the head.

4. Break off a piece of the roll. Brush one side of it with egg and stick it to the bear's face. Pinch it to make it look like a snout.

5. Cut two small pieces for the ears and four bigger ones for the legs. Pinch them into position under the bear's body and head.

6. Using the kitchen scissors or a knife, snip or score the ends of the bear's legs to make them look like paws with claws.

24

Letting the bears rise

7. Make all the bears this way. Cover them loosely with a tea towel and leave them in a warm place* to rise for about an hour, until they have doubled in size. Then brush them lightly with beaten egg to glaze them, and use currants to make their eyes. Now you can add other decorations if you like.

cooking the bears

8. 🍴 Bake the bears in the oven (see page 21) for 20–25 minutes, depending on their size, until they are golden brown. Then put them on to a wire rack to cool.

MUMMY BEAR

Currants for eyes

Mummy bear was brushed with beaten egg, and then sprinkled with sesame seeds.

DADDY BEAR

Currants for eyes

BABY BEAR

Currants for eyes

Daddy bear was brushed with beaten egg, and then sprinkled with grated cheese.

Baby bear was brushed with beaten egg, and then decorated with poppy seeds.

*Ask an adult for a suitable, warm place.

25

Fruity bread

A Christmas wreath not only tastes good; it looks really festive too! Here you can see all you need to make a fruity bread wreath. The wreath will rise more quickly if you put it in an oiled plastic bag and then leave it in a warm place. Turn the page to see how to make the icing and marzipan for your wreath.

You will need

75 ml (3 fl oz) warm milk

25 g (1 oz) butter

1 small egg

½ teaspoon salt

25 g (1 oz) soft brown sugar

225 g (8 oz) strong white flour

1. Set oven to 200°C/400°F/ Gas Mark 6. Put the sugar, flour, yeast, salt, spice, and cinnamon in the bowl and stir together.

2. Add the butter and cut it up. Rub everything together with your fingertips until the mixture looks like fine breadcrumbs.

3. Add the fruit, egg, and milk. Mix them together to make a ball of dough. Knead the dough on a floured surface for five minutes.

1 sachet easy blend yeast

15 g (½ oz) mixed peel

1 teaspoon ground cinnamon

40 g (1½ oz) currants

½ teaspoon ground mixed spice

4. Roll the dough into two sausages about 60 cm long. Put the sausages side by side and twist them together.

5. Bend the twist into a ring on the baking tray. Wet the ends of the twist with water and stick them together.

6. Leave the ring in a warm place until it has doubled in size. Bake it for 20 to 25 minutes, then move it on to a wire rack, to cool.

A christmas wreath

Turn your fruity wreath into a Christmas treat with a tangy lemon icing and some marzipan leaves and berries. You can use ready-made marzipan, or the fondant icing used on page 8.

25 g (1 oz) marzipan (for holly leaves)

15 g (½ oz) marzipan (for holly berries)

1 tablespoo lemon juice

You will need

12 drops of green food colouring

12 drops of red food colouring

175 g (6 oz) icing sugar

colouring marzipan

Make a hole with your finger in the marzipan and add the food colouring. Knead the marzipan until it is an even colour.

Holly leaves

Roll the green marzipan out on a sugared surface until it is 3mm thick. Cut out leaves with the cutter (or a knife).

Holly berries

Take small pieces of red marzipan and roll them into balls with your fingers. Try to keep all the balls the same size.

making icing

1. Sift the icing sugar into the small bowl. Add the lemon juice and stir with the wooden spoon until the icing is smooth.

2. Spoon the icing along the top of the wreath and let it drip down the sides. Decorate the wreath before the icing sets.

The finished christmas wreath

Marzipan holly leaves

Marzipan holly berries

Serve the ring cut into wedges with some berries and leaves on each wedge.

Snowy white icing

*Use a knife if you can't find any cutters.

speedy pizza

This pizza is quick and easy to make. Here you can see how to make the pizza and sauce, and on the next page are some ideas for toppings. You can make two 10 cm (4 in) pizzas from the ingredients below.

You will need

150 g (6 oz) self-raising flour

A pinch of salt

3–4 tablespoons milk

50 g (2 oz) grated cheese

40 g (1½ oz) butter

COOK'S TOOLS

Mixing bowl

Small saucepan

Wooden spoon

Rolling pin

Cheese grater

Knife

Chopping board

Baking tray

For the Sauce

1 small onion

1 dessertspoon tomato purée

A pinch each of salt and pepper

1 small tin of tomatoes

Make sure that an adult helps you when you are using a sharp knife.

making the sauce

1. Set the oven at 220°C/425°F/Gas Mark 7. Peel the onion, then cut it in half, and chop it up finely on the chopping board.

2. Put the chopped onion in the saucepan. Add the tomatoes, tomato purée, salt and pepper, and stir the mixture together.

3. Cook the mixture over a low heat for about 15 minutes, stirring from time to time. Then turn off the heat and let it cool.

making the dough

1. While the sauce is cooking, make the dough. Put the flour, salt and butter in the mixing bowl. Cut the butter into small pieces.

2. Rub the pieces of butter into the flour between your fingertips and thumbs until the mixture looks like breadcrumbs.

3. Add the grated cheese and milk to the flour mixture. Mix everything together until you have a smooth ball of dough.

4. Divide the dough in two and make each piece into a ball. Roll each ball of dough into a circular shape about 10 cm (4 in) across.

5. Lay the circles of dough on the greased baking tray. Spoon the tomato sauce on them, spreading it out evenly to the edges.

6. Decorate the pizzas (see next page). Put them in the oven to cook for 15–20 minutes, until the edges are golden brown.

Now turn the page.

party pizzas

Once you have made the basic pizzas – and before you cook them – you can turn them into picture pizzas, using any of the ingredients below. Try making one of the pizzas shown here, or experiment with ideas of your own.

Grated cheese

Sliced ham cut into strips

Sliced peppers

Topping ingredients

Stoned black olives

Cheese sliced then cut into shapes

Sliced cooked sausage

Italian pizza

Chopped ham

Chopped red pepper

Sliced cooked sausage

Sliced mushrooms

Sweetcorn

Tinned sweetcorn

Sliced mushroom

Grated cheese

Chopped green pepper

Mouse pizza

Slices of cheese

Black olives

Sliced-mushroom ears

Green pepper whiskers and mouth

Stars-and-stripes pizza

Tinned sweetcorn

Strips of sliced ham

Sliced cheese cut into stars

Clock pizza

Green pepper hands

Grated cheese

Half an olive

Black olives

Sliced cooked sausage

33

cheesy potato boats

Stuffed potatoes are a meal in themselves and are easy to make. Here are some fun ideas on how to decorate them once you have cooked them. Potatoes take a long time to cook, so put them in the oven 1 to 1½ hours before you want to eat them.*

For two people you will need

2 knobs of butter

50 g (2 oz) grated cheese

1 large scrubbed potato

Stoned black olives

Ideas for decoration

Button mushrooms

Strips of cucumber

Sliced cheese cut into shapes

Carrots, sliced o cut into sticks

COOK'S TOOLS

Small bowl

Knife

Fork

Tablespoon

Cheese grater

Greased baking tray

Sliced peppers, cut into strips

Shredded lettuce

Watercress

cooking the potatoes

1. Set the oven at 200°C/400°F/ Gas Mark 6. Prick the potatoes and place them on the greased baking tray. Bake for 1¼ hours.*

2. When cooked, cut the potatoes in half lengthways. Scoop out the middles into the bowl and mash them. Stir in the butter and cheese.

3. Spoon the mixture back into the potato skins and level them off. Then put them back into the oven for another 15 minutes.

*Ask an adult to check if the potatoes are cooked. Leave the oven on for step 3.

Decorating the potatoes

You can decorate the potatoes once they are cooked. Make them into sailing boats, steamer ships, or rowing boats as shown here.

sailing jacket

Yellow pepper flag

Cocktail-stick mast

Cheese sail

Red pepper deck

Rowing boat

Carrot oars

Cucumber oars

Black olives

Stuffed steamer

Watercress steam

Funnels made of sliced carrot and mushroom stalks

Red pepper

Shredded lettuce for sea

35

perfect pastry

Here and on the next five pages you can find out how to make mini fruit tarts and savoury quiches. These two pages show you how to make the pastry cases. These quantities will make about thirty small tarts, depending on the size of the tins you use.

You will need

25 g (1 oz) caster sugar (for sweet tarts only)

About 3 tablespoons water

100 g (4 oz) margarine or butter

A pinch of salt

COOK'S TOOLS

Mixing bowl

Knife

Fork

Rolling pin

Wooden spoon

Pastry cutter

Greased patty tins or little tartlet tins

Wire rack

225 g (8 oz) plain flour

making the pastry

1. Turn the oven on to 200°C/400°F/Gas Mark 6. Put the flour, butter and salt in the mixing bowl. Cut up the butter.

2. Rub the flour and butter together with your fingertips until they look like breadcrumbs. For sweet tarts, add the sugar.

3. Now mix in the water, a little at a time. You should have a soft ball of dough that leaves the sides of the bowl clean.

4. Sprinkle flour on to the table and your rolling pin. Put the dough on to the table and roll it out until it is quite thin.

5. Cut circles out of the pastry, using a pastry cutter or cup. The circles should be a bit bigger than your tart tins.

6. Lay each circle of pastry over a tin. Gather in the edges and press the pastry into place so that it fits the tin.

For sweet tarts

7. Prick the bases of the pastry cases with a fork. Put them in the oven and bake them for 15 minutes, until golden brown.

8. Let the tins cool, then lever the pastry cases out with a knife, and put them on a wire rack. See how to fill them over the page.

For savoury tarts

9. Add the filling now (see pages 40–41). Then put the tarts in the oven to bake for about 20 minutes, until the filling sets.

Turn to the next four pages for filling ideas.

Fruit tarts

To make these fruit tarts, cook the pastry cases first (see the previous page). Then fill them with fruit and glaze them with melted jam. It is best to use soft fruits like those shown below, because you don't have to cook them.

Cooked, sweet pastry cases

You will need

450 g (1 lb) fruit, such as:

Tinned or fresh pineapple

Raspberries

Blackberries

Seedless grapes

COOK'S TOOLS

Small saucepan

Knife

Wooden spoon

Pastry brush

Tinned mandarin oranges

100 g (4 oz) redcurrant jelly (or sieved apricot jam)

Filling the tarts

1. Make a glaze for the tarts by melting the redcurrant jelly or sieved apricot jam in the small saucepan over a low heat.

2. Brush the insides of the pastry cases with the glaze. Wash the fresh fruit, drain the tinned fruit, and cut the grapes in half.

3. Arrange the fruit in the pastry cases, as shown below. Then brush the fruit with the glaze, which will set as it cools.

The finished tarts

This tart has a ring of blackberries with a raspberry in the centre.

Arrange mandarin orange segments so they overlap to form a circle.

Use slices of grape, four pineapple segments, and a grape for the centre.

Use pineapple, mandarin segments, raspberries, and halved grapes.

The grape in the centre of this is put between two chunks of pineapple.

This one has mandarin orange segments and blackberries.

mini quiches

When making quiches or savoury tarts, put the filling in the pastry cases before you cook them. Add whatever you want to the basic filling of eggs and milk to get any flavour you like. Try combinations of the ingredients shown below.

You will need

200 ml (⅓ pt) milk

2 eggs

Uncooked, unsweetened pastry cases (see pages 36–37)

Chopped spring onions

Plus any of these ingredients

Sliced tomatoes

Strips of sliced ham

Finely sliced leeks

Sliced mushrooms

Grated cheese

Tinned tuna fish

COOK'S TOOLS

Knife

Fork

Cheese grater

Chopping board

Measuring jug

What you do

1. Slice the tomatoes and mushrooms. Chop the ham and spring onion. Drain the tuna. Grate the cheese.

2. Break the eggs into the measuring jug. Beat them well with the fork. Pour in the milk and whisk the mixture together.

3. Arrange the fillings in the pastry cases, pour on the egg mixture. Put them in the oven for 20 minutes (see page 37).

The finished quiches

This quiche is filled with a mixture of tuna fish and spring onion.

Place sliced leeks in this quiche. Then put strips of ham on top.

Tinned tuna fish and sliced tomatoes are used in this quiche.

This quiche is topped with grated cheese and sliced tomatoes.

In these two quiches, sliced mushrooms are arranged to overlap slightly.

sweet and savoury scones

Here you can find out how to make sweet scones, fruit scones, and cheese scones. The ingredients shown will make about ten scones. Below you can see how to make sweet, fruit, and cheese scone doughs. Turn the page to find out how to cut out and fill your scones.

You will need

120 ml (4 fl oz) milk

50 g (2 oz) sultanas

50 g (2 oz) grated cheddar cheese

making scone dough

1. Set the oven to 425°F/220°C/ Gas Mark 7. Put the flour and salt in the mixing bowl. Add the butter and cut it into pieces.

2. Rub the butter and flour together with your fingertips until the mixture looks like breadcrumbs. Stir in the sugar.

3. Add the milk to the mixture and stir everything together with the wooden spoon to make a smooth mixture.

42

Baking tray
Wire rack
Mixing bowl
Whisk
6 cm biscuit cutters
Measuring jug
Rolling pin
Sharp knife
Cheese grater
Pastry brush
Wooden spoon

225 g (8 oz) self raising flour

25 g (1 oz) caster sugar

50 g (2 oz) softened butter

A pinch of salt

Fruit scones

Cheese scones

4. Knead the mixture by pressing and squeezing it together with your hands until you have formed a stiff dough.

5. Follow the recipe for sweet scones but add the sultanas to the mixture after you have stirred in the sugar.

6. Follow the same recipe for sweet scones, but add the grated cheese instead of the caster sugar before you add the milk.

teatime treats

You can use different shaped biscuit cutters to make small scones, or make a big scone round with your hands. Scones taste best when warm, with or without butter. Try filling sweet or fruit scones with jam and whipped cream.

COOK'S TOOLS

Small bowl   Whisk

Sharp knife

Knife

You will need

Jam

Cutting out the scones

1. Grease a baking tray. Gently roll out the dough until it is 2 cm thick. Cut out shapes with biscuit cutters dipped in flour.

2. Put the scones on a baking tray*, brush them with milk and bake for 12 to 15 minutes, until firm and risen. Cool them on a wire rack.

A scone round

3. Roll the dough into a circle 2.5 cm thick. Divide the top into eight, then brush it with milk. Bake for about 25 minutes.

Whipping the cream

4. Whisk the cream in the small bowl until it is thick. Cut the sweet or fruit scones in half and fill them with jam and cream.

*Sprinkle some extra grated cheese on top of the cheese scones.

150 ml (¼ pint)
double cream

SWEET SCONES

Strawberry jam

Whipped cream

CHEESE SCONES

A FRUIT SCONE ROUND

*Grated cheddar cheese
sprinkled on before baking*

Simple Shortbread

Two-tone shortbread biscuits are great fun to make and eat. On this page you can see everything you will need to make plain and chocolate shortbread dough. The ingredients shown below make enough shortbread for eight owl's eyes, eight lollipops, and twelve window biscuits. Look on the next page to find out how to make each biscuit and to see the finished results.

For plain shortbread

125 g (4 oz) softened butter

50 g (2 oz) caster sugar

You will need

COOK'S TOOLS

Pastry brush

Knife

2 greased baking trays

Mixing bowl

Rolling pin

Wire rack

Wooden spoon

Palette knife

Lollipop sticks

Sieve

15 g (½ oz) cocoa powder

blanched almonds

175 g (6 oz) plain flour

For chocolate shortbread

125 g (4 oz) softened butter

50 g (2 oz) caster sugar

160 g (5 ½ oz) plain flour

3 tablespoons milk

2. Add 125 g (4 oz) butter, cut up. Rub the flour, sugar and butter together with your fingers until the mixture is like breadcrumbs.

1. Set the oven to 350°F/180°C/ Gas Mark 4. Sieve 175 g (6 oz) flour into the mixing bowl. Stir in 50 g (2 oz) of sugar.

3. Add a tablespoonful of milk to the mixture. Mix everything together with your hands to form a ball of dough.

making chocolate shortbread

1. Sift 160 g (5½ oz) flour and the cocoa powder together. Make the chocolate dough in the same way as the plain dough.

2. Divide each ball of dough into three equal pieces. You will need one plain and one chocolate piece to make each type of biscuit.

47

Biscuit bazaar

Owl's eyes

1. Roll a piece of each type of dough into a square 15 cm by 15 cm. Brush the top of each square with milk.

2. Put the square on top of another and roll them up together. Then cut the roll into 16 slices, as shown.

3. Stick two slices together with milk to make each biscuit. Put the biscuit on a baking tray. Add an almond beak to each one.

Lollipops

1. Roll out the chocolate dough into a square 10 cm by 10 cm. Make the plain dough into a roll 10 cm long with your hands.

2. Brush the chocolate square with milk and wrap it round the plain roll. Squeeze the ends of the chocolate dough together.

3. Cut the roll into eight slices. Put the slices on to the baking tray and push a lollipop stick into the middle of each one.

Windows

1. Shape the two sorts of dough into rectangles 4 cm by 9 cm with your hands. Cut them in half lengthways.

2. Stick two strips of plain and chocolate dough together with milk. Stick the other two strips on top of them, as shown.

3. Cut the block of dough strips into 12 square slices with a sharp knife. Put the slices on to a baking tray.

cooking the biscuits

Bake the biscuits in the top half of the oven for 15 to 20 minutes until they are a pale gold colour. The lollipop biscuits are thicker and will take slightly longer to cook. When the biscuits are done, carefully move them from the baking trays and put on a wire rack to cool and harden.

storing your biscuits

Biscuits go soggy if they are left out for too long. Store them in an airtight tin or jar to keep them fresh and crunchy.

The finished biscuits

OWL'S EYES

LOLLIPOPS

WINDOWS

Puff pastry

You can make lots of mouth-watering pastries with ready-made puff pastry. Here you can find out how to make Eccles cakes, palmiers (palm tree-shaped pastries), and cheese twists. The ingredients are enough to make about 30 pastries. Turn the page to see the finished results.

You will need

350 g (12 oz) ready-made puff pastry

1 egg

50 g (2 oz) demerara sugar (for palmiers)

½ teaspoon caster sugar (for Eccles cakes)

¼ teaspoon ground nutmeg (for Eccles cakes)

15 g (½ oz) soft butter (for Eccles cakes)

COOK'S TOOLS

Measuring jug Baking tray Small bowl

10 cm plain biscuit cutters Wire rack

Rolling pin

Wooden spoon Fork

Knife Pastry brush

15 g (½ oz) demerara sugar (for Eccles cakes)

15 g (½ oz) mixed peel (for Eccles cakes)

25 g (1 oz)
chopped roasted
hazelnuts (for palmiers)

50 g
(2 oz)
grated
cheddar
cheese (for
cheese twists)

40 g (1½ oz) currants (for
Eccles cakes)

What to do

1. Set the oven to 220°C/425°F/ Gas Mark 7. Grease a baking tray with some butter. Beat the egg in a jug with a fork.

2. Put the pastry on a floured surface and divide it into three equal pieces. You will need one piece of pastry for each recipe.

Eccles cakes

1. Roll out the pastry on a floured surface until it is 3 mm thick. Cut out six circles with the plain biscuit cutter.

2. Put the currants, peel, butter, 15 g (½ oz) demerara sugar, and nutmeg in a small bowl and mix them together.

3. Put a teaspoon of mixture in the centre of each circle. Brush the circle with egg and pinch the edges together.

4. Turn the parcels over and press them flat. Cut two slits in the top. Brush them with egg and sprinkle caster sugar on top.

pastries on parade

Hazelnut palmiers

1. Roll out the pastry into a rectangle 30 cm by 20 cm. Brush it with egg and sprinkle on two thirds of the sugar and nuts.

2. Fold the short sides of the rectangle into the middle. Brush them with egg and sprinkle with the rest of the sugar and nuts.

3. Fold the folded edges into the middle. Brush the top with egg. Fold the pastry in half to form a roll. Cut it into 16 slices.

cheese twists

1. Roll out the pastry into a rectangle 25 cm by 20 cm. Brush it with egg. Sprinkle the cheese over half of the rectangle.

2. Fold the pastry over the cheese to make a sandwich and roll it flat. Trim the edges with a knife. Brush the sandwich with egg.

3. Cut the sandwich lengthways into 20 strips Twist each strip several times and press the ends on to the baking tray.

Baking the pastries

Bake the pastries on a greased baking tray. Cheese twists and palmiers should be baked for 10 minutes and the Eccles cakes for 15 minutes. The pastries are ready when they are crisp and golden brown. Put the cooked pastries on a wire rack to cool. Pastries taste best on the day they are made, so you can eat them as soon as they are cool!

The finished pastries

ECCLES CAKES

HAZELNUT PALMIERS

CHEESE TWISTS

pastry in a pan

Choux pastry* is great fun to make as it puffs up to two or three times its size when you bake it. Here and on the next five pages, you can find out how to make and decorate lots of different choux cakes. The ingredients shown below will make about five spiders, snakes, puffs and éclairs, and lots of worms.

You will need

¾ teaspoon salt

100 g (3½ oz) butter

4 eggs

150 g (5 oz) plain flour

1 beaten egg

250 ml (8 fl oz) water

COOK'S TOOLS

Wooden board   Small bowl   Sieve   Saucepan   Measuring jug

Baking tray   Piping bags with sizes 0, 2, 6, and 8 plain nozzles   Wire rack   Cocktail sticks

Fork   Pastry brush   Wooden spoon

*Choux is French for puff.

What to do

1. Set the oven to 200°C/ 400°F/ Gas Mark 6. Grease the baking tray. Sieve the flour into the small bowl.

2. Put the water, salt and butter into the pan and heat them gently until the butter has melted and the mixture begins to bubble.

3. Remove the saucepan from the heat and stand it on a wooden board. Add all the flour to the mixture in one go.

4. Beat the mixture vigorously until it comes away from the sides of the saucepan. Leave it to cool for one to two minutes.

5. Beat the eggs in the small bowl. Add them to the mixture a little at a time until it is smooth and shiny.

6. Fit a nozzle* into the piping bag. Put the bag in the measuring jug and fold its top over the sides. Spoon in the mixture.

7. When the bag is full, twist the top to close it. To start piping, squeeze the pastry down through the nozzle.

8. Pipe your shapes on to the greased baking tray and brush them with beaten egg. Bake them for 20 to 25 minutes until golden.

9. Remove the shapes from the oven and prick each one with a cocktail stick. Place the shapes on a wire rack to cool.

Turn the page to see which nozzle to use to pipe each shape.

Light as air

You can pipe choux pastry into any shape you like. Follow the instructions at the bottom of the page to make spiders, snakes, worms, puffs, and éclairs. When the shapes are cool, fill them with whipped cream and top them with the chocolate icing shown opposite.

You will need

100 g (4 oz) cooking chocolate

100 g (4 oz) icing sugar

Puffs

To make puffs and spiders' bodies, use the size 8 nozzle and pipe small, round piles on to the baking tray.

Snakes

Use the size 6 nozzle to make the snakes. Start at the head of the snake and pipe a wiggly line for its body.

Spiders' legs

Pipe the spiders' legs using the size 0 nozzle. Make four left legs and four right legs for each spider.

Worms

These are piped with a size 2 nozzle. Pipe the worms as though you are writing commas.

25 g (1 oz) butter

300 ml (½ pint) double cream

COOK'S TOOLS

Whisk   Sieve

2 small bowls

Wooden spoon

Palette knife

3 tablespoons water

Eclairs

Eclairs are made with the size 8 nozzle. Pipe 5 cm lines of pastry for mini éclairs and 10 cm lines for big ones.

What to do

1. Whisk the cream in a small bowl until it is thick and fluffy. Slice the puffs and éclairs in half and spoon the cream into them.

2. Cut the butter and chocolate into pieces. Put them in the saucepan and stir them together over a low heat until they melt.

3. Stir in the water. Remove the mixture from the heat. Sift the icing sugar and then add it to the mixture. Stir until smooth.

4. Spread icing along the buns, éclairs, and snakes with a palette knife. Dip the worms in the icing with your fingers.

57

Choux Show

Here are some ideas for decorating your choux shapes. The spider's web was made by piping some of the chocolate icing on to a large white plate. Try piping other animals to make a choux zoo for a special tea or party.

The finished cakes

Currants

Red liquorice

Sugar balls

Sugar strands

Snakes

The snakes are filled with cream and topped with chocolate icing. Try making a family of snakes.

Current and cream eyes

Red liquorice forked tongue

Sugar strand markings

Spiders

To make spiders, cut some puffs in half and fill them with cream. Arrange four legs on each side of the spiders and pipe more cream on top. Add currants for eyes.

Worms

The worms have been dipped in chocolate icing and then covered in sugar balls before the icing set.

Sugar balls

Eclairs

Chocolate éclairs are topped with a thick layer of chocolate icing and filled with lots of whipped cream.

Puffs and profiteroles

Choux puffs can be eaten like little cakes as shown here, or as a delicious dessert, filled with cream and covered in lots of chocolate icing.

59

Fruit fools

You can make fruit fools with any fruit soft enough to mash with a fork. Here you can see how to make strawberry or banana fool. The amount of fruit shown for either sort will make four small fools.

You will need

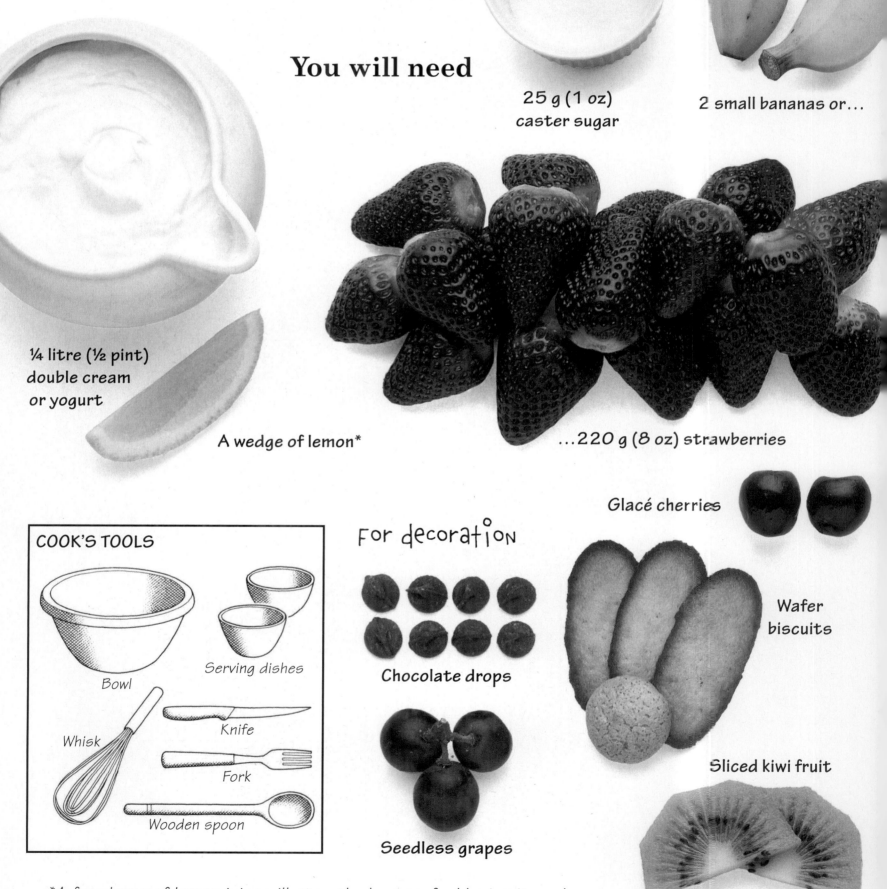

25 g (1 oz) caster sugar

2 small bananas or...

¼ litre (½ pint) double cream or yogurt

A wedge of lemon*

...220 g (8 oz) strawberries

Glacé cherries

COOK'S TOOLS

Bowl

Serving dishes

Whisk

Knife

Fork

Wooden spoon

For decoration

Chocolate drops

Wafer biscuits

Seedless grapes

Sliced kiwi fruit

*A few drops of lemon juice will stop the banana fool losing its colour.

what you do

1. Cut the strawberries in half, or peel and slice the bananas. Put the fruit in the bowl and mash it with a fork until it is smooth.

2. Whisk the cream or yogurt until it is thick and creamy. Add this and the sugar to the mashed fruit. Stir them in well.

3. Pour the fruit mixture into the serving dishes or glasses. Decorate them as shown below, or however you like.

BEAR FOOL

CAT FOOL

FLOWERING FOOL

The banana-fool bear has biscuit ears, eyes made of biscuits and chocolate drops, a cherry nose, and a slice of kiwi fruit for a mouth.

The flower pattern on this strawberry fool is made of sliced kiwi fruit and glacé cherries arranged around a grape in the middle.

The strawberry-fool cat has sliced strawberry ears, eyes made of grapes, a biscuit and chocolate-drop nose, and whiskers made of kiwi fruit.

61

chocolate dips

You can make delicious homemade sweets by dipping your favourite fruits and nuts into melted chocolate. Make sweets out of the things shown below and put them in pretty sweet papers to give away as presents. You can also use them to decorate a special cake, or best of all – just enjoy eating them!

You will need

150 g (6 oz) plain chocolate

Cherries

Mandarin segments

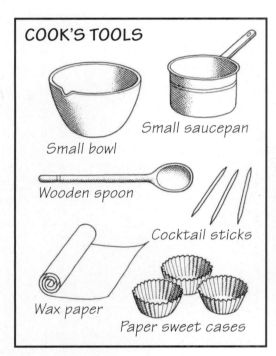

COOK'S TOOLS

Small bowl

Small saucepan

Wooden spoon

Cocktail sticks

Wax paper

Paper sweet cases

Brazil nuts

Blanched almonds

Walnuts

melting the chocolate

1. Break the chocolate up into a bowl. Heat some water in the saucepan on a low heat until it just begins to bubble.

2. Stand the bowl over the saucepan on a low heat. Stir the chocolate with a wooden spoon until it completely melts.

3. Turn off the heat. Very carefully move the saucepan and the bowl from the stove to a mat or tea towel.

Strawberries

Seedless grapes

Dipping the fruit and nuts

4. One at a time, put a fruit piece on a cocktail stick and dip half of it into the chocolate. Then put it on wax paper to dry.

5. Using your fingers, dip the nuts halfway into the melted chocolate, one at a time. Let them dry on the wax paper.

Arranging your sweets

You can put the finished sweets in paper sweet cases. If they are for a special occasion, arrange them in circular patterns on a large plate.

The finished sweets

making meringues

Meringues are deliciously sweet and crunchy and are made from only the whites of eggs, some sugar, and a little salt. Separating the egg white from the yolk is quite tricky because yolks break very easily, so always start with more eggs than you need! Be very careful not to allow any yolk to mix with the egg whites, or the recipe won't work. Meringues take five hours to cook because they have to be baked in a cool oven to keep them white.

COOK'S TOOLS

Baking tray — Jug — Cup — Mixing bowl

Baking parchment — Teaspoon — Palette knife

Tablespoon — Whisk

Small bowl — Sharp knife — Scissors

You will need

A pinch of salt

2 eggs

100 g (4 oz) caster sugar

Glacé cherries

Currants

Candied orange peel

64

What to do

1. Set oven at its lowest setting. Cut out a square of parchment the same size as the baking tray. Put it on top of the baking tray.

2. *Crack one egg in half and pour the yolk from one half of the shell into the other, letting the egg white fall into the jug.

3. Tip the yolk into the cup and the white into the small bowl. Do the same thing again to separate the second egg.

4. Add a pinch of salt to the egg whites in the small bowl. Beat the egg whites with the whisk until they form stiff peaks.

5. Whisk the sugar into the egg whites a little at a time, until you have used all the sugar and the meringue looks glossy.

Nests

6. Shape a heaped tablespoonful of meringue into a circle on the baking tray. Make a hollow in the middle with a teaspoon.

Ghosts

7. Spread tablespoonfuls of meringue into ghost shapes with a teaspoon. Cut pieces of glacé cherry to make eyes.

Snowmen

8. Use a teaspoonful of meringue for the head and a tablespoonful for the body. Decorate with pieces of currant, candied peel and cherry.

9. Bake the meringue ghosts, snowmen and nests slowly for four to five hours until firm. Put them on a wire rack to cool.

*Ask an adult to help you with this.

Snow-White Surprises

Meringue nests make mouth-watering desserts when they are filled with cream and fruit. Use soft fruits and arrange them in patterns on the cream-filled nests. You could make nests at Easter, and fill them with chocolate eggs, or make ghosts for a Hallowe'en treat. Snowmen are great fun as Christmas decorations that you can eat!

You will need

Glacé cherries

Tinned mandarin segments

Seedless black and green grapes

120 ml (4 fl oz) double cream

Strawberries

Tinned peach chunks

Filling the nests

1. Pour the cream into a small bowl. Whisk the cream until it is thick and fluffy and forms soft peaks.

2. Cut off all the strawberry stalks. Slice some of the strawberries and cut others into quarters with a sharp knife*.

3. Spoon the whipped cream into the nests and arrange the pieces of fruit in pretty patterns on top of them.

*Ask an adult to help you.

66

The finished meringues

MERINGUE NESTS

Slice of strawberry

Pieces of glacé cherry for eyes

GHOSTS

Piece of strawberry

Peach chunk

Black grape

Mandarin segment

Whipped cream

Glacé cherry

Green grape

SNOWMEN

Nose made from a triangle of candied peel

Slice of glacé cherry for a mouth

Currant eyes

Currant buttons

Ice cream Sundaes

Ice cream sundaes are great fun to make. All you need is ice cream, some sauces, and lots of tasty things to put on top. You must make sundaes quite fast, so that they don't melt. Put them in the fridge as you finish them, or eat them at once!

COOK'S TOOLS

2 small bowls

Wooden spoon

Knife

2 big spoons

Sieve

Glasses or dishes

Small saucepan

You will need

Vanilla ice cream

Chocolate ice cream

Strawberry ice cream

For decoration

Chocolate sugar strands

Sugar strands

Mixed nuts

Wafer biscuits

Chocolate drops

Liquorice

Chopped or sliced fresh fruit

making the sauces

For raspberry Sauce

150 g (6 oz) raspberries (frozen or fresh)

75 g (3 oz) caster sugar

Raspberry Sauce

1. Wash the raspberries and put them in a sieve over a bowl. Then push them through the sieve using a wooden spoon.

2. Add the caster sugar to the raspberry pulp a little at a time. Then stir the sauce vigorously until all the sugar has dissolved.

For chocolate Sauce

100 g (4 oz) plain chocolate

chocolate Sauce

1. Break up the chocolate. Put it in the bowl with the water. Heat some water in the saucepan until it gently bubbles.

2. Place the bowl over the saucepan until the chocolate melts. Turn off the heat and stir the chocolate until smooth.

3 tablespoons water

spicy biscuits

You can make spicy biscuits in all kinds of different shapes. You can make them for parties or just for tea. The ingredients shown here will make about twenty-five biscuits. On the next four pages you can find out how to cut out and decorate your biscuits.

You will need

75 g (3 oz) butter

275 g (10 oz) plain flour

making the biscuit dough

1. Set the oven at 170°C/ 325°F/Gas Mark 3. Sift the flour, baking powder and cinnamon into a mixing bowl. Stir in the sugar.

2. Add the butter and cut it up. Rub the flour and butter together with your fingertips until the mixture looks like breadcrumbs.

3. Break the egg into a jug and beat it with a fork. Add the golden syrup and mix it with the egg until smooth.

1 dessertspoon
cinnamon

1 level teaspoon
baking powder

COOK'S TOOLS

Mixing bowl

Wooden spoon

Rolling pin

Measuring jug

Sieve

Biscuit cutters

Knife

Fork

Palette knife

Baking tray

100 g (4 oz) soft brown sugar

50 g (2 oz) golden syrup

1 small egg

4. Make a hollow in the flour and pour in the egg mixture. Mix everything together well until you have a big ball of dough.

5. Put the ball of dough into a plastic bag. Place it in the fridge for 30 minutes, which will make it easier to roll out.

6. Sprinkle some flour on a table, and on your rolling pin. Roll out the dough evenly until it is about 0.5 cm (¼ in) thick.

Decorative biscuit shapes

cutting out the dough

1. Use biscuit cutters to make different shaped biscuits. To do this, press the cutter into the dough, then lift the cutter off.

2. With a palette knife, lift each biscuit on to the baking tray. (If they won't all fit, bake the biscuits in two batches.)

3. Decorate the biscuits now, as shown below. If you want to ice the biscuits, leave them plain when you cook them.

Decorating your biscuits

Use different cutters for the biscuits. They can be shaped like people, stars and the moon, or even dinosaurs. Here are some ideas for how to decorate them.

uncooked biscuits

You will need

Glacé cherries

Walnuts

Sesame seeds

Currants

Blanched almonds

72

Turn the page to find out how to ice the biscuits.

cooking the biscuits

4. Put the baking tray on a high shelf in the oven. Bake the biscuits for 15–20 minutes, until they are golden brown.

5. When cooked, take the biscuits out of the oven and move them on to a wire rack. They will harden as they cool.

Arranging your biscuits

Make a family of biscuit people and line them up, or use a blue plate as a pond for some ducks or as a sky for lots of stars.

The finished biscuits

easy icing

To make fancier biscuits you can
ice them before decorating them.
You must cook the biscuits plain
and make sure that they have
cooled completely before icing
them. Below you can find out
how to make white icing and
chocolate-flavoured icing.

COOK'S TOOLS

Sieve

Small bowl

Knife

Wooden spoon

You will need

25 g (1 oz) cocoa powder
(for chocolate icing only)

1 tablespoon hot water

100 g (4 oz) icing sugar

Glacé cherries

making the icing

1. Sift the icing sugar into the
small bowl. Add the water a little
at a time, mixing it with the
sugar to make a smooth paste.

2. To make chocolate icing, use
75 g (3 oz) icing sugar and 25g
(1 oz) cocoa powder and make it
the same way as the white icing.

3. Spoon a little icing on to each
biscuit and spread it out evenly
with a wet knife. Don't worry if
it dribbles down the edges a bit.

74

decorating the biscuits

Before the icing sets, decorate your biscuits with any of the things shown below. You can make patterns on them, or decorate them to look like faces or animals. Here are some ideas to try.

Chocolate drops

Coloured chocolate sweets

Chocolate sugar strands

Sugar strands

peanut butter cookies

These mouth-watering cookies are very quick and easy to make. Crunchy peanut butter makes the cookies very nutty, but use smooth peanut butter if you prefer it. Bake the cookies for 15 minutes if you like them soft in the middle, or for 20 to 25 minutes if you like them crisp. Store the cookies in an airtight tin to keep them fresh.

You will need

125 g (4 oz) crunchy peanut butter

175 g (6 oz) soft brown sugar

1 egg

125 g (4 oz) soft butter

175 g (6 oz) self-raising flour

COOK'S TOOLS

2 teaspoons

Wooden spoon

Mixing bowl

Wire rack

Knife

Greased baking tray

What to do

1. Set the oven to 350°F/180°C/ Gas Mark 4. Cut up the butter in the bowl and add the sugar. Beat them together until fluffy.

2. Add the peanut butter, flour, and egg, and beat everything together with the wooden spoon until the mixture is smooth.

3. Put teaspoonfuls of mixture on to a baking tray. Bake the cookies for 15 to 25 minutes*. Then put them on a wire rack to cool.

The finished cookies

*See the introduction to this recipe.

chocolate brownies

Chocolate brownies are a great American treat. They are crisp on the outside, but wonderfully soft and chewy inside. Below are all the ingredients you need to make dark chocolate and walnut brownies. On the next page you will find the finished brownie squares.

COOK'S TOOLS

Shallow baking tin   Wire rack   Saucepan   Mixing bowl

Small bowl   Scissors   Fork   Greaseproof paper   Wooden spoon   Knife

You will need

175 g (6 oz) soft brown sugar

65 g (2½ oz) butter

50 g (2 oz) plain chocolate

What to do

1. Set the oven to 180°C/350°F/ Gas Mark 4. Cut a square of greaseproof paper and put it in the bottom of the greased baking tin.

2. Heat some water in the saucepan until it just starts to bubble. Put the butter in the small bowl and cut it up.

3. Break up the chocolate into the bowl and stand it over the pan. Stir the butter and chocolate together until they have melted.

65 g (2½ oz)
walnut pieces

2 eggs

65 g (2 oz)
self-raising flour

4. Break the eggs into the mixing bowl and beat with a fork. Add the flour, walnuts and sugar and mix with the wooden spoon.

5. Pour the melted chocolate and butter into the mixture in the bowl and beat them hard until the mixture is smooth.

6. Pour the mixture into the baking tin and bake for 30 to 35 minutes. Leave it to cool in the tin and then cut it into squares.

A brownie pack

Brownies can be made with any kind of chocolate or nut. Try using white or milk chocolate instead of dark chocolate and using other sorts of nut, such as hazelnuts, peanuts, or almonds instead of walnuts.

The finished brownies